ASTRONAUTS

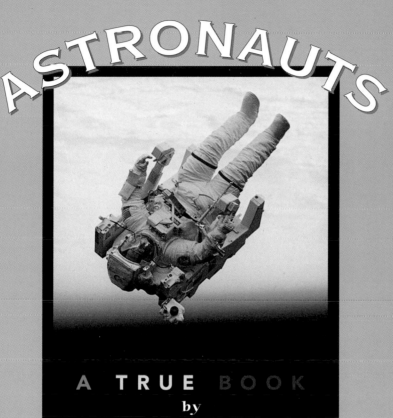

A TRUE BOOK

by

Allison Lassieur

Children's Press®

A Division of Grolier Publishing

New York London Hong Kong Sydney
Danbury, Connecticut

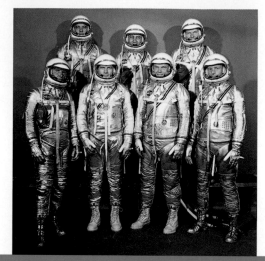

In 1959, these seven men were chosen as the first American astronauts.

Subject Consultant
Peter Goodwin
Science Department Chairman
Kent School, Kent, CT

Reading Consultant
Linda Cornwell
Learning Resource Consultant
Indiana Department
of Education

The photograph on the cover shows one of the crews that flew aboard the Space Shuttle Atlantis in 1996. The photo on the title page shows astronaut Bruce McCandless during a space-walk in 1984.

Visit Children's Press® on the Internet at:
http://publishing.grolier.com

Library of Congress Cataloging-in-Publication Data

Lassieur, Allison
    Astronauts / by Allison Lassieur.
       p. cm. — (A true book)
    Includes bibliographical references and index.
    Summary: Describes how astronauts are trained and how they live and work in space and discusses some famous male and female astronauts.
    ISBN: 0-516-22000-4 (lib. bdg.)   0-516-27185-7 (pbk.)
    Astronautics—Juvenile literature. 2. Astronauts—Juvenile literature.
[1. Astronautics. 2. Astronauts.] I. Title. II. Series.

TL793 .L2935 2000
629.45—dc21
                                                                99-055981
                                                                    CIP

GROLIER
PUBLISHING

Contents

In 1962, John Glenn boarded *Friendship 7* and became the first American to orbit Earth (above). In 1998, he made history again by becoming the oldest person to fly in space (right).

Humans in Space

Have you ever heard the names Neil Armstrong, John Glenn, Sally Ride, or Mae Jemison? All of these people have one thing in common. They all had one of the most exciting and dangerous jobs in the world. They were astronauts.

Yuri Gargarin was launched into orbit on April 12, 1961. He will always be remembered as the first human in space.

The word astronaut comes from two Greek words that mean "star sailor." In 1961, a Russian man named Yuri Gagarin became the first person to blast into space. Less than a month later, Alan Shepard became the first American to fly in space.

Today, there are 141 U.S. astronauts, and even more are in training. They travel aboard

The thirty-one men and women shown in this photograph hope to become astronauts one day. Do they have what it takes to make it through training?

a spacecraft called a Space Shuttle. A Space Shuttle can blast into space and fly back to Earth. It lands like an airplane.

Being an astronaut is hard work. Each space flight has different goals, and every astronaut has a special job to do. They do science experiments to learn how the human body reacts to being in space. They release satellites into space. Some of these satellites help predict the weather. Others beam telephone messages

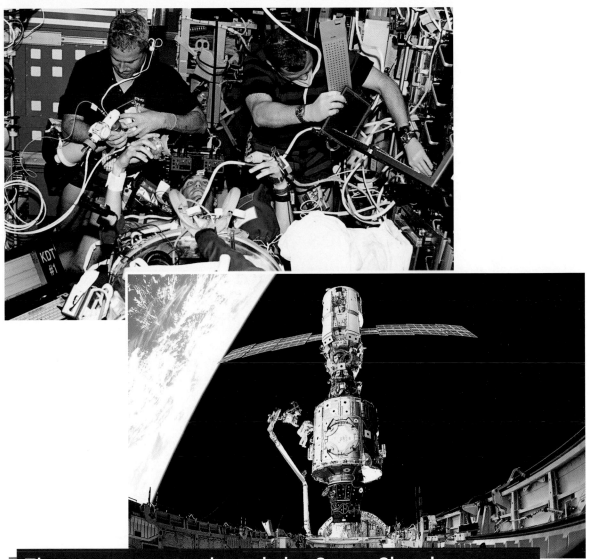

These astronauts aboard the Space Shuttle *Columbia* are conducting experiments to find out how the human body reacts to the weightlessness in space (top). Astronauts spend months learning how to build and repair space objects. These two astronauts are working on part of the International Space Station (bottom).

from one part of the world to another. Still others take pictures of Earth.

Sometimes astronauts fix broken satellites. Astronauts on the Space Shuttle have also delivered supplies to astronauts living on space stations. Astronauts are now helping to build a new International Space Station where people from different countries can live and work together for long periods of time.

When the Hubble Space Telescope was released in 1990, it did not work. Astronauts had to repair it in space. This photo was taken from inside the Space Shuttle.

Astronauts in the Past

In the 1950s and 1960s, scientists in the United States and the former Soviet Union competed to launch the first person into space. The Soviets won that race in 1961. Yuri Gagarin flew around, or orbited, Earth once. A few months later Alan Shepard flew into

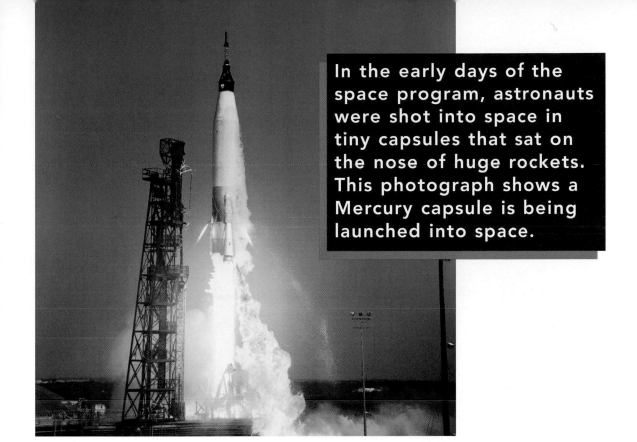

In the early days of the space program, astronauts were shot into space in tiny capsules that sat on the nose of huge rockets. This photograph shows a Mercury capsule is being launched into space.

space aboard a Mercury spacecraft. His flight lasted only 15 minutes. He did not fly all the way around Earth. In 1962, astronaut John Glenn became the first American to orbit Earth.

The Gemini program proved that humans could spend time in space. This photograph shows *Gemini 8* blasting into space.

The Mercury program included four more successful space flights. Next came the Gemini program (1964–1966). One of

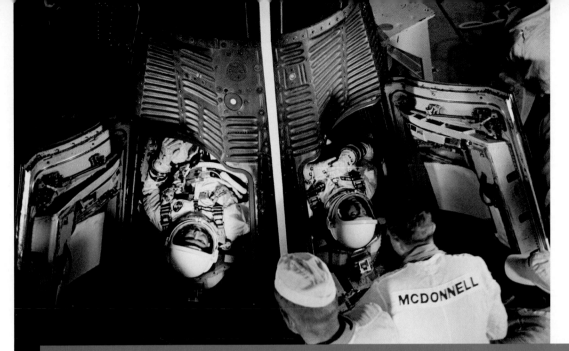

Just before *Gemini 5* was launched, scientists at NASA checked out the capsule and the two astronauts, Leroy Cooper and Charles Conrad.

the main goals of the Gemini flights was to find out how long people could survive in space. In 1965, astronauts Leroy Cooper and Charles Conrad stayed in space for 8 days.

Scientists at NASA (National Aeronautics and Space Administration) realized that people could live in space without any trouble. It was time to send astronauts to the Moon.

Finally, NASA began the Apollo program (1967–1972). Astronauts on the first Apollo flights tested all the procedures needed to go to the Moon. On July 20, 1969, Neil Armstrong and Buzz Aldrin,

Astronaut Neil Armstrong took this picture of fellow astronaut Buzz Aldrin. If you look closely, you can see Armstrong's reflection in the helmet.

two astronauts on *Apollo 11*, became the first people to set foot on the Moon.

Eleven other lucky Americans also had a chance to walk on the Moon. Some drove across the Moon's rocky surface in a rover. A few even played golf while they were there! No one can say the astronauts never had any fun.

Since the Apollo program ended in 1972, the United States has not sent any more astronauts to the Moon. The trips were very expensive and most Americans had lost interest in Moon missions.

In 1972, astronaut Eugene Cernan took a ride on the Moon in this rover.

Women Astronauts

In the 1950s, when NASA was looking for the first astronauts, some women applied for the job. A few made it through training, but NASA

The first women accepted into NASA's astronaut program were (from left to right): Rhea Seddon, Sally Ride, Kathryn Sullivan, Shannon Lucid, Anna Fisher, and Judith Resnik.

refused to accept them. Finally, in 1978, six women were accepted into NASA's astronaut program. Sally Ride was one of those women. In 1983, she became the first U.S. woman in space. Soon, even more women

Sally Ride talks to ground controllers from the flight deck of the Space Shuttle *Challenger.*

joined the space program. In 1992, Mae Jemison became the first African-American woman on a Space Shuttle crew. In 1999, a pilot named Eileen Collins became the first woman to command a Space Shuttle mission.

Mae Jemison was a doctor before she became an astronaut.

In 1996, Shannon Lucid spent 188 days on the Russian space station Mir. No other American astronaut has stayed in space that long. When Lucid returned to Earth, President Bill Clinton awarded her the Congressional Medal of Honor.

Shannon Lucid lived on Russia's Mir space station for more than 6 months. This photograph shows her exercising on a treadmill.

Astronaut Training

Today's astronauts go through a hard training program. First, they must spend several weeks in class studying everything from space science to math. Next, they go through survival training. They learn things like how to stay alive if their spacecraft splashes back

Eileen Collins, the first female Space Shuttle commander, goes through water survival training school in Pensacola, Florida.

to Earth in the ocean instead of on land.

One of the most important parts of astronaut training is

learning about weightlessness. On Earth, the force of gravity keeps us from floating in the air. In space, gravity is not strong enough to hold an astronaut's feet on the floor. The astronauts feel like they weigh less than they do on Earth.

Astronaut trainees practice living and working in space by spending time in a huge, deep tank of water. Floating in water is almost like floating in space.

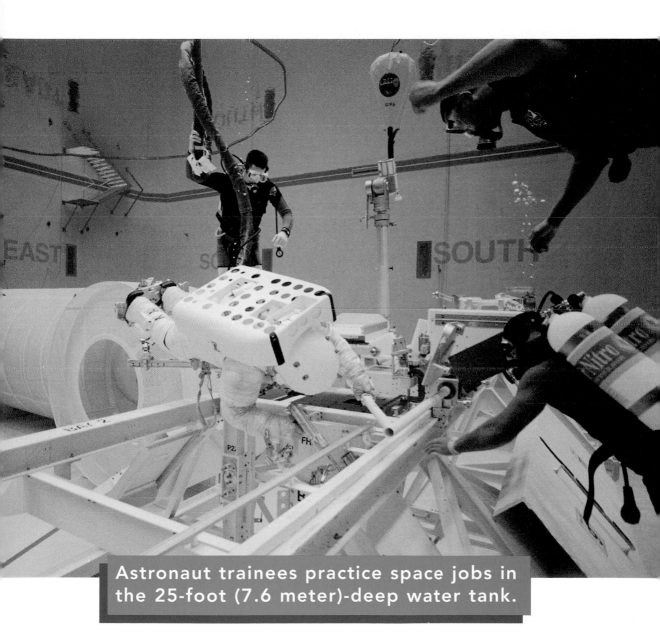

Astronaut trainees practice space jobs in the 25-foot (7.6 meter)-deep water tank.

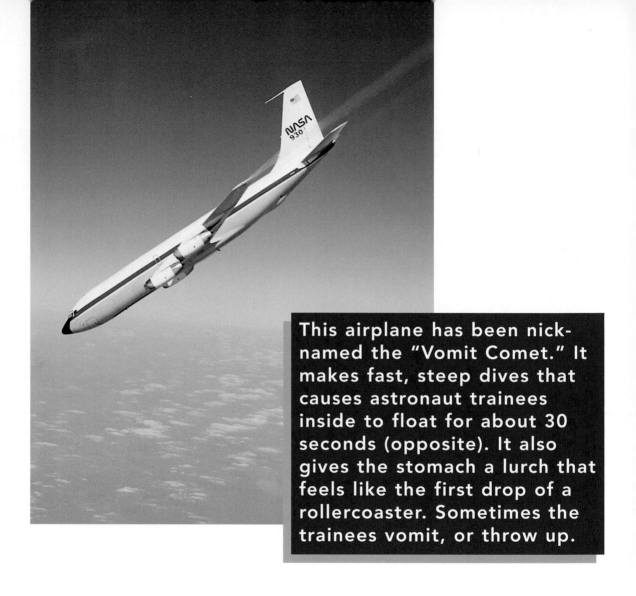

This airplane has been nick-named the "Vomit Comet." It makes fast, steep dives that causes astronaut trainees inside to float for about 30 seconds (opposite). It also gives the stomach a lurch that feels like the first drop of a rollercoaster. Sometimes the trainees vomit, or throw up.

Trainees also learn about weightlessness by riding in a special airplane. The plane

climbs thousands of feet into the air, then dives straight toward Earth. This steep dive creates a few seconds of weightlessness inside the airplane.

This model of the Space Shuttle looks exactly like the real thing. Astronauts use it during training.

After all that, it is time for flight training. Astronauts practice flying a model of the Space Shuttle. They control the model spacecraft from a flight deck with the same switches, dials, and displays as the real Space Shuttle.

Astronauts in Space

You eat and sleep every day, and so do astronauts. In the 1960s and 1970s, eating in space was not much fun. Food came in freeze-dried bricks, gooey tubes, and even bite-sized cubes covered with gelatin. The food was easy to eat, but not very tasty.

This is the food that the *Apollo 11* astronauts had to look forward to. These bricks of food include: chicken and vegetables (left), beef hash (center), and beef and gravy (right).

Today's shuttle astronauts eat real food with real silverware. They get three meals a day— plus snacks. Everything comes in a package with a Velcro base

that sticks to their meal tray. The meal tray has straps that the astronauts can attach to the walls of the Space Shuttle. That way they can eat while they are floating.

Space Menu

Today, astronauts eat the same foods they might eat in their kitchen at home. Of course, the view out the window is different!

Astronaut Loren Shriver chases down some weightless candies on the flight deck of the Space Shuttle *Atlantis*.

For breakfast, an astronaut might eat scrambled eggs, sausage, a sweet roll, peaches, an orange drink, and cocoa. Lunch might include a ham and cheese sandwich, cream of mushroom soup, stewed tomatoes, a banana, and some cookies. For dinner, the menu could be beef with mushrooms, broccoli with cheese, strawberries, pudding, and cocoa.

Astronaut Kevin Kregal takes a nap aboard the Space Shuttle *Discovery*.

When astronauts need a rest, they can either sleep in their seats or strap themselves into one of the sleeping bags attached to the walls of the shuttle. During long missions, astronauts sleep in special bunks. These bunk beds are different from the ones at summer camps on Earth. One astronaut sleeps on the top bunk and another sleeps on the bottom bunk. A third astronaut sleeps upside down on the underside of the lower bunk—facing the floor!

When astronauts work outside the spacecraft, they wear spacesuits made of tough

Astronaut Mark Lee's space suit keeps him comfortable and warm in space.

material. These suits are like the ones some underwater divers wear. It is very cold in space, so space suits help keep astronauts warm. There is no air in space, so astronauts breathe air from tanks they carry with them. Without these space suits, astronauts would die.

Going to the bathroom in space is a lot like going to the bathroom on Earth. Space toilets look a lot like Earth toilets.

This toilet (left) and shower (right) are just like the ones astronauts will use onboard future space stations.

When an astronaut flushes, air sucks everything into special containers. The containers are thrown out when the shuttle returns to Earth.

Working in Space

An astronaut's day in space is different from a day at work on Earth, but astronauts have just as much to do. Each member of the crew has a special job.

The commander/pilot is the boss. He or she is in charge of the mission and the safety

Shuttle pilot Rick Husband looks over the flight data aboard the Space Shuttle *Discovery*.

of the crew. The commander flies the Space Shuttle and controls its huge robot arm. The arm is used to launch and grab satellites.

The mission specialist makes sure all the shuttle equipment is working. He or she also handles day-to-day life on the shuttle. Mission specialists plan

Mission commander Kent Rominger (left) and mission specialist Ellen Ochoa (right) use a laptop computer on the *Discovery*'s flight deck.

what jobs the crew members will do each day. They also get to go on space walks outside the shuttle.

The payload specialist is in charge of any special experiments or cargo aboard the shuttle. This person does not have to be an astronaut, but he or she does have to be approved by NASA. Payload specialists have special skills and training.

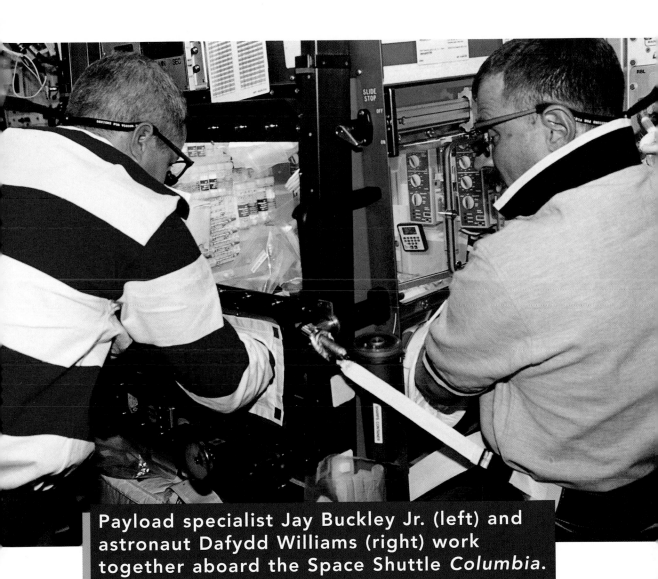

Payload specialist Jay Buckley Jr. (left) and astronaut Dafydd Williams (right) work together aboard the Space Shuttle *Columbia*.

To Find Out More

Here are more places to learn about astronauts, the shuttle, and the Moon missions:

 **Books**

Briggs, Carole. **Women in Space.** Lerner Publications, 1999.

Collins, Michael. **Flying to the Moon: An Astronaut's Story.** Sunburst, 1994.

Kettelkamp, Larry. **Living in Space.** Morrow Junior Books, 1993.

Maze, Stephanie. **I Want to Be an Astronaut.** Harcourt Brace, 1999.

Sakurai, Gail. **Mae Jemison: Space Scientist.** Children's Press, 1996.

Organizations and Online Sites

National Aeronautics and Space Administration (NASA)

http://www.nasa.gov

This site has plenty of information about space travel, from the Moon missions to life on the Space Shuttle.

http://spacelink.nasa.gov

This online library has all kinds of space information.

http://www.jsc.nasa.gov

A kids' link from this site includes other links to great space sites, including information about the Moon station and missions to Mars.

National Air and Space Museum

Smithsonian Institution
601 Independence Ave. SW
Washington, DC 20560
http://www.nasm.si.edu/

Visit the museum's great website for information about exhibits and special programs.

Windows to the Universe

http://windows.engin.umich.edu/

This site features information about the planets, the solar system, space history, and astronauts.

Important Words

astronaut a person who travels in space

freeze-dried a way of preserving food

gravity a force that pulls objects toward one another

orbit to travel around an object

satellite an object that orbits Earth

velcro piece of fabric with small hooks that attach to another piece of fabric with small loops. It is used to attach or close things.

Index

Meet the Author

Allison Lassieur is the author of more than a dozen books for young readers. She enjoys writing about health, history, world cultures, current events, and American Indians. She has also written magazine articles for *Disney Adventures*, *Scholastic News*, *Highlights for Children*, and *National Geographic World*.

When Ms. Lassieur is not writing, she enjoys reading, playing with her spinning wheel, and participating in historical reenactments.